In a word . . .

Anneke Kaai
and
Eugene H. Peterson

PARACLETE PRESS
Brewster, Massachusetts

piquant

Copyright © 2003 by Anneke Kaai and Eugene H. Peterson

This edition copyright © 2003 by Piquant

The right of Anneke Kaai and Eugene H. Peterson to be identified as authors of this work has been asserted by them in accordance with the Copyright, Designs and Patents Act, 1988.

First edition 2003

09 08 07 06 05 04 03 7 6 5 4 3 2 1

Published by Piquant, PO Box 83, Carlisle, CA3 9GR, United Kingdom

E-mail: info@piquant.net

Website: www.piquant.net

ISBN 1-903689-21-X

Copublished in the United States by Paraclete Press, Brewster, Massachusetts

Website: www.paracletepress.com

ISBN 1-55725-351-X

Also published in Dutch as *Bijbelwoorden in beeld* (Boekencentrum, 2003)

A library catalogue record of this book is available in the UK from the British Library and in the USA from the Library of Congress.

Cover image: Anneke Kaai, *Blessing*

Photographs by Werner Aerne Zwitserland (Kaai) and Kate French (Peterson)

Design: Jonathan Kearney, pool31

Contents

Author's Preface

Word and image go together in any pursuit of understanding in the
Christian faith. Our fundamental Word, after all, became
incarnate, visible and tactile, in Jesus. Word and image really
cannot be separated, even though we try it
often enough. Word without image easily
evaporates into an abstraction; image
without word can degenerate into an idol.
Word and image need each other. And so
artists have always held a prominent
place in bringing the message of the
gospel to life and making it personally
present to us. Especially when a word
goes flat through repetition and familiarity, image brings the
imagination into play and sharpens our awareness of and
participation in the word and the Word-made-flesh.

I have long admired Anneke Kaai's work for using color and
form to pull us into a deeper perception of and participation
in the Creed, the Psalms, and now these individual biblical
words. So I was delighted when I was invited to offer my
responses to her paintings of these words, words that are so
very important to the way we live our lives, paintings that
provoke responsive emotions appropriate to the words
themselves. It became an act of prayer for me to sit silently
before these paintings and try to express a fuller sense of
what living each of these words involves for me,

EUGENE H. PETERSON

Dedicated to my father on the occasion of his 90th birthday—
with deep appreciation for the wisdom with which he and my
mother encouraged me to develop the talents God gave me.

Artist's Introduction

With this, the publication of my fifth art book, *In a Word*, and the second in association with an English text by Eugene H. Peterson, I am filled with deep joy and thankfulness towards God. *In a Word* contains well-known words from the Bible that evoke associations, memories and sometimes strong emotions, words like "love," "grace," and "eternity." These words have long fascinated and inspired me, and it has been an adventure to immerse myself in them over the last three-and-a-half years, the time it has taken to complete these 23 paintings. I delved into the core meaning of each word and then interacted with it in a direct, spontaneous way in order to give it a contemporary  "body"—I have particularly tried to express the range of emotions evoked by these words, from the dynamic rush of "resurrection" to the tranquillity found in "peace."

The style of these works is symbolic–abstract, for the linear, the plastic, and the painterly aspects have symbolic value. I have purposely chosen for centered, restful compositions. The cross is a recurring symbolic form, because biblical imagery is so irrevocably tied to Christ's death.

The paintings are all in the format of 80–110, in acrylic on Plexiglas. The thick application of sharp, primary colors has been significant: layer upon layer was added, sometimes only to be removed again, whereby the works gained in "durability."

I have included short descriptions of the works in the back of the book which include a Bible verse that I have added subsequently. The descriptions are also available in French, German, Dutch and Spanish on the website at www.boekencentrum.nl

ANNEKE KAAI

Love

Love is the primary word given to guide us into the best that we can ever hope to receive or give. It is, at the same time, the word most frequently associated with betrayal and disappointment and lies. Complicating things even further, it is a word terribly vulnerable to cliché, more often than not flattened into non-meaning by chatter and gossip. I use the word easily and often, but too often it is a cover for lust, infatuation, and fantasized romantic ecstasies. I say "love" but what I mean is "I want . . . I desire . . . I need . . ." Even as I say it, I know that it is not love. It is all me-directed. It is all self. The largeness of love is reduced to the mouse hole of the ego. The fire of love is smothered under blankets of self-preoccupation. How do I recover its glory, its splendor, its energy?

Going to a dictionary is a poor way to look up the meaning of a word, any word, but especially a word that comes into our lives in the life and language, death and resurrection of Jesus. So instead of reaching for the dictionary, we look to the Story, the God Story as told in Jesus.

God is love. And I am not. So I will no longer look to the dictionary or my own experience for the meaning but to the Story. As I assimilate the Story, slowly, meditatively, believingly, I begin to get it: every act of love requires personal, sacrificial giving appropriate to the person being loved; the less of me, the more of God—and God is love.

Grace

"Is the world a friendly place?" Albert Einstein thought that the way we answer that question shapes the way we live. The prominence and frequency of the word "grace" in Christian discourse is our answer: "Yes, the world is a friendly place." God is revealed in every dimension as being for us, not against us, inviting us into his ways, not rejecting or scorning us, speaking our names in recognition, not ignoring or dismissing us. The good, the true, and the beautiful that God intends for us is not rationed out bit by bit; it is a torrent, poured into our lives. This is the witness of our Scriptures, the story of Jesus, and the experience of a grand company of "sinners saved by grace." Goodness comes to us unbidden, unasked for, previous to our asking or needing. What would we have known to ask for? This is amazing grace.

But it takes considerable getting used to. The stories we grow up with, the schools that teach us, the images that define our society, and the careers we pursue don't prepare us to live in a world of grace. They train us to "get ahead," to "look out for number one," to "make the most of yourself" in a world in which "there is no free lunch." Grace if anything is a mere "grace note," superfluous to the so-called "real world." And if we are unable or unwilling to enter the fray, we are told that there is nothing for us but to be consigned to the mediocrities of a passive consumer.

So we require continual reorientation through worship and prayer if we are to live appropriately in this "friendly place" permeated by God's grace. We need help in slowing down so that we have the leisure to observe what is being given. We need detoxification from addictions that turn neighbors into targets for our lust or rivals in avarice. We need protection from distractions so that we can be present to the Unseen, to the God who gives so continuously and generously. "Grace is everywhere" (Bernanos) so there's no excuse. In the rush to get ahead, the greatest loss is to miss seeing the immense glory of where we are, who we are.

Happiness

Arms lifted high towards heaven, open to what we cannot grasp, receptive to God, our lives a chalice into which God pours grace— this is the posture of the happy man, the happy woman. But the pursuit of happiness, an absolute fundamental in the "bill of rights" of so many, ends up in a labyrinth of frustration. That which completes us can only be received, never pursued or hunted or grasped. And God is the giver.

Arms lifted cannot be used to hold onto people or things. Arms lifted are useless for defense or assault. Arms lifted, hands open, upturned faces release us from an obsessive preoccupation with what we can get and hold onto. We are disarmed, and cannot hysterically protect our interests or fight for our rights.

This is not difficult to understand for we have continuous evidence of it every day in the air that we breathe, the sun that warms us, the beauty that surrounds us, to say nothing of our bodies that we did not conceive, our souls that we did not make, our salvation that we did not earn. All the same, it is difficult to imagine and live for we are continuously bombarded with urgent appeals to acquire and compete, to take and get, to buy and sell. The wisdom of giving and receiving is not on conspicuous display in our world. Which, of course, is why the happiness quotient is so low in so many lives.

Receiving is the only life-form congruent with grace and the happiness inherent in it. God gives; this is basic to everything that we know about God, everything that Jesus reveals to us about God. We can't "get" God or what God gives. If we want to get in on God, we can only do it by receiving: lift up your arms!

Holiness

Life is messy. Some of the mess is made by others, but each of us is responsible for a good bit of it on our own through our indecisiveness, our sloppy moral housekeeping, our groveling in the muck of self-pity, our bossy interference in other lives, our refusal to pick up after ourselves, dumping the garbage of our emotions and betrayals and cynicism in the backyards of our neighbors. But beyond the mess we catch occasional glimpses of order and proportion, clean lines, cool clarity, and colors that invite repose and beauty. Holiness.

But holiness is not simply good housekeeping, an obsessive cleanliness that keeps everything in its place, bans dogs and children, and conducts all conversations in a whisper. It is not moral fussiness. It is not being nice.

To understand and participate in holiness we go to the source: God is holy. Holiness, therefore, must refer to what is alive, whole, vibrant, personal, and relational. Maybe even a little reckless. All of which God is. And God wants us in on his holiness. Anything that suggests lifeless perfection or depersonalized abstraction, like the neatly kept parlor in which no one is free to laugh or slouch, is simply wrong. God lives, and we are most alive in his presence.

God doesn't abandon us to our mess-making; God comes to us in Jesus and leads us into the clean, light-filled world of God's holiness where all lines of relationship and purpose are clear; he invites us to live holy lives in his holy presence. Disgust (or despair) over our messed-up lives is replaced with deep reverence as we participate in this so much larger and more bracing reality of God's holiness.

Wrath

Wrath virtually always feels righteous. Which, of course, is why it is so dangerous. The energies of wrath put us on a warpath for the rights of men and women who have been wronged, or ignite a passion to defend ourselves when we perceive that we have been wronged. When we are angry we feel more alive, caring about things that matter, about wrongs committed whether done to another or to me. But a wrong. And what can be wrong about doing my energetic and passionate best to right the wrong?

But however noble our wrathful determination to set wrongs right, wrath is a blind guide in the pursuit of right. When we "see red" we are prevented from seeing souls. And when our fist is clenched it is incapacitated as a helping, outreaching hand. Still, it feels so right, so urgent, so black and white, so, well, godlike. Besides, what about the wrath of God? Doesn't God's anger legitimate mine? Not at all. Whatever the wrath of God involves, it is way beyond our competence to engage in it. He has made it clear that he will take care of everything in that department.

Our anger-fueled attempts to right wrongs inevitably damage the soul being "fixed." Doing the right thing in the wrong way always compounds the wrong. For wrong is never just a "wrong"—a person with an eternal soul is involved in that wrong and that person can only be set right by love and grace and forgiveness, the way Jesus did it on the cross. That is why Jesus commands us to love and pray for our enemies. It is the only thing that we can be trusted to do with them that doesn't do more harm than good.

(un)Righteousness

Things fit together. Weather and trees, oceans and fish, flowers and soil—and men and women, children and parents, friends and guests. God and the world and us: righteousness, right relationships, right for one another, right with God. And God, in and behind it all, right and setting things right with us in Jesus.

Or not. For righteousness insofar as we have anything to do with it, means that we participate in God's righteousness. We can't do it on our own; we don't have it in us. And when we do try to do it on our own, it quickly turns into self-righteousness, which in turn quickly turns into the unrighteousness that destroys right relationships and results in oppression, arrogance, greed, and a hundred variations on idolatry. The evidence of God's righteousness, God's essential rightness in putting things and us right, is in what he does as he makes and forgives, blesses and provides. When we attempt to dismiss God or live in defiance of him, we violate the fundamental righteousness in which God works. And when we try to do the works of God without God, we mess them up badly, both the works and the people involved.

The essential thing to observe in all aspects of righteousness is that there is no "right" or "righteousness" apart from relationships derived from God relationships. Righteousness is not a static thing, not an abstraction, nothing otherworldly. It is formed in the thick of living, on the streets and in the neighborhoods, in kitchens and supermarkets, hoeing potatoes and fixing flat tires, writing a check and receiving a blessing. None of us are right in and of ourselves. We are right only in God, whose righteousness takes place in the community of Father, Son and Holy Spirit and is revealed in everything we see and experience in creation, salvation, and holy living.

Reconciliation

"Bury the hatchet . . . Kiss and make up . . . Let bygones be bygones
. . . Shake hands and get on with it . . . Wipe the slate clean . . . "
We use such phrases to smooth over differences when we reach
an impasse in a quarrel, or step in to separate two boys headed
for a fistfight. The frequency with which the phrases are used is
a sign of how often we don't get along with one another.

It's true. We don't get along with one another. We never have.
And we aren't getting any better. Cain started it off by killing
his brother, and we've been at it ever since. Not always killing
but using not quite so lethal tactics on those we disagree with
and dislike: yelling and cursing, pushing and shoving,
snubbing and ignoring, divorcing and dismissing. We want
them out of our lives. Sometimes the dislike reaches a
national level and we go to war.

Despite century after century of accumulating wisdom and
knowledge, breakthroughs in the arts of healing and the
insights of psychology, the spread of major religions
worldwide, and periodic peace conferences led by
experienced diplomats, our recently completed twentieth
century ended up being the most fractious and bloodiest
of the lot. The suffering is incalculable. Century after
century we are getting better at making war and worse at
making peace.

Maybe this is because we start at the wrong end; we attempt
to resolve differences by going after the people who offend us
instead of the God whom we offend. But our failure to get
along with one another has its roots in our failure to get along
with God. So what do we do? Wrong question. The question is
"what has God done?" And the answer is that God has already
done everything necessary for us to get along with him and
each other (but first him) by giving us Jesus. Reconciliation
begins at the cross of Jesus. But it doesn't stop there; now we are
in on it. Every reconciled Christian is a recruit peacemaker.

Power (of the Evil One)

The Good, the True, and the Beautiful are everywhere present in our lives—in our world! The very fabric of life is woven from them, a storied tapestry resplendent in color and dance, play and delight. The cosmos is good and true and beautiful: heaven and earth, elephants and whales, Arcturus and falcons, roses and iguanas. To say nothing of men and women made in the image of God. God is good, creation is true, we are beautiful. So why isn't everything OK?

Why do we keep running into the evil, the false, and the ugly? Where do they come from? We ourselves are certainly responsible for some evils, a great many even. But not all. Evil power wars against God's creation, salvation, and blessing. It mangles and destroys, seduces and takes possession. Biblical writers have given this power a variety of names, none of them human: serpent, dragon, demon, Devil, Satan, Rahab, Leviathan, Behemoth, Belial, Beelzebub, Antichrist. These are obviously not euphemisms; the names recognize the existence of the evil power, however it appears, as evil—alien and hostile to life. But the designations also give boundaries to evil. Evil is not a vague, nameless miasma seeping into our lives from who knows where. If we can identify evil power for what it is, as evil, we are able to resist and oppose it. We know what we are dealing with.

We are no better than others in providing answers to "why evil?" Our expertise, if you can call it that, is in facing and dealing with the evil power. We have strong and, to us, incontrovertible evidence that Jesus is on the front lines in dealing with the evil power. His sacrificial death on the cross 2000 years ago was the decisive victory over evil that will be finalized at the Last Judgment. Our faithful prayers in Jesus' Name enlist us as participants in the dismantling of the evil powers.

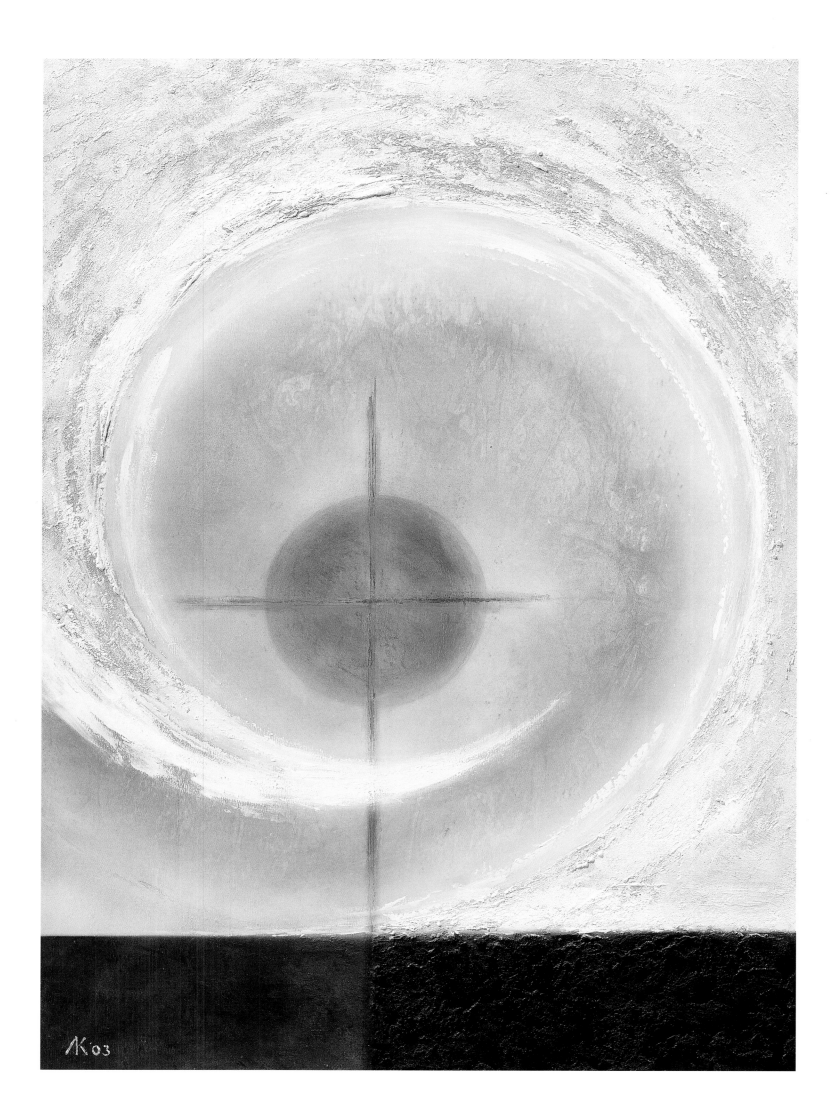

Power (of God)

We come across the phrase "the power of God" and start thinking of power in general—horsepower, atomic power, nuclear power, military power, political power (and, more frivolously, power lunches, power naps, power ties, power walks). We read into the word someone or something that overpowers.

But that is not the way the power of God works. It is never employed impersonally. God is person in relationship; his power is never an impersonal force. One of our early church pastors said, "Coercion is no attribute of God" (Irenaeus). We have to inhabit the story of God's revelation if we are to discern how God uses power. The power of God certainly means the ability to make things happen in an extraordinary way, but bullying force isn't part of it. It is certainly not what takes place when a fuse ignites a stick of dynamite (named after the Greek word for power, *dynamis*). The power of God is always exercised in personal ways, creating and saving and blessing. It is never an impersonal application of force from without.

The Gospel story of Jesus tested by the Devil in the wilderness contrasts the right and wrong ways of employing the power of God. The three tests that the Devil puts to Jesus all have to do with exercising the power of God: turn stones into bread, rule the world, perform a spectacular miracle by leaping off the pinnacle of the temple. All three involve doing something both good and godly: feeding hungry people, ruling the nations justly, advertising the miraculous ability of God right there on the streets of Jerusalem. But each also involved using God's power impersonally, the power of God separated from a relationship with God. When Jesus left the wilderness of temptation, St. Luke tells us that he returned to Galilee to take up his work of teaching and healing "in the power of the Spirit" (Lk. 4:14), work that he carried out exclusively in personal relationships of love and grace, forgiveness and blessing.

Sin

A hundred years ago, a London newspaper asked several well-known public figures to each write an 800-word essay on the topic "What's Wrong with the World." Among those invited was the popular Fleet Street journalist, G. K. Chesterton. In response he wrote a one-word essay: "Me." What's wrong with the world? "Me."

Others wrote about poverty and economics, war and peace, ignorance and education, sickness and health, mediocrity and eugenics. And of course they each had a proposal on how to set right what is wrong with the world.

Only Chesterton came up with the obvious, which also happens to be the Christian answer: me. Identifying what is wrong with the world with "me" is a personal way of saying, "sin."

The proposals set forth by the other writers were intelligent and well informed. Some were brilliant. But they were also impersonal, dealing with programs or plans that would redistribute income, enact legislation, develop mechanisms or tools, and reform the educational system. None of them was without merit. Any one of them would have helped, some in substantial ways. But not one was personal. None identified the core "wrong," the man or woman who refuses, whether in ignorance or willfulness, to deal relationally and responsibly with what is "right" with the world, namely, God. They missed the biblically defined sin-target, me.

We are created to live in relationship and responsibility with one another and with our Creator and Savior. When we don't do it, it soon becomes apparent that there is something "wrong with the world" and somewhere in that "wrong" there is a "me." That's the place to start doing something about it.

Forgiveness

How does it happen that Jesus Christ, in his sacrificial death on the cross, takes care of my sins? Takes care of and sorts out all the intricately tangled lines of sin, knotted and snarled in a dizzying accumulation of wayward emotions, mean actions, blasphemous thoughts, prideful pretensions, ranging along the extensive waterfront of the seven "deadlies" (pride, anger, avarice, lust, sloth, gluttony, greed). And not only my sins; the sins of the whole world.

Forgiveness, accomplished by Jesus on the cross, is the deepest mystery. The artist's colors and forms hint at what eludes description in prose. The storyteller awakens echoes of feelings or memories long buried. We need all the help we can get. But the mystery remains—and deepens: the Gospel-narrated stories and our prayerful meditations on that crucifixion lead us gently but surely into a way of life in which we are set free of guilt: "Your sins are forgiven." Period.

We are free of debilitating self-loathing. Free of the exhausting pose of pretending perfection. Free of the bullying emotions of blame. No prison time. No leftover accusations. No probation. No lingering recriminations.

The mystery deepens: we find that we are also able to forgive those who have sinned against us. What Jesus did on the cross for us makes it possible for us to extend forgiveness to others. The great mystery of forgiveness—wrongs made right with a word, the guilt of sin wiped out in a stroke, the death of Jesus becoming life for us—can be extended in what we do and say in Jesus' name. The grass is green.

Forgiveness must never be trivialized. The mystery must ever be respected. It looks easy. It is not easy. An enormous sacrifice made this possible. An unimaginable death set this in motion. Sacrifice cost nothing less than everything. And "Jesus paid it all."

Salvation

Salvation is our biggest word. It is impossible to exaggerate the historical significance and the endless personal ramifications of salvation. It exceeds our powers of understanding. We will never get our minds around it. But we see well enough what is going on: Doors open! We see God at work! God heals and helps, forgives and blesses, takes a creation in ruins because of human willfulness and then patiently begins to make a new creation of it, takes a world corrupted by evil and begins the long, slow work of transforming it into a holy place.

We see all this in bits and pieces, moments and fragments. It is understandable that we often reduce salvation to a handful of these moments and fragments. But we must not. We are dealing with God's work in history on a scale of comprehensiveness that ever eludes us.

But if we can't overstate the significance of salvation we can certainly misconstrue it. We can read our own ideas into what we think salvation ought to be. We can spin escapist fantasies of salvation that project either our ignorance or our sin (usually both) onto a large screen of desire. When we do that we incapacitate ourselves from entering the actual salvation that God is working right now all around and in us. We also commonly end up with a lot of frustration or bitterness when we find that God doesn't do all the things that we imagined he must do if he is any kind of God at all.

Keep your eyes on those doors. As the doors slide apart, meditatively read the Story (Ex. 1–19), the grounding salvation story that is given its definitive form in Jesus Christ (Mk. 1–16).

Conversion

"Walking down a road" is a common metaphor for living. Living means going someplace, heading towards a destination. Roads and highways, trails and paths lead somewhere. Isaiah and John the Baptist prepared "the way of the Lord" (Is. 40:3; Mk. 1:3). A psalmist sang of the good fortune of the person "in whose heart are the highways to Zion" (Ps. 84:5). Jesus identified himself as a road to walk on ("I am the way . . ." Jn. 14:6). The Way is a metaphor for the Christian life in the story of the early Christians as told in the Acts (19:9; 24:14).

But not everyone is walking down this road. Some of us lose our way, taking the wrong road out of ignorance, bad advice, or carelessness. As we spend our lives trying this road or that, but always arriving at dead-ends or going in circles and never getting anywhere, at some point we realize that we don't know where we are going. When we realize that we are lost and going "nowhere," and are given directions for getting on the road of life, the obvious thing to do is simply to turn around and head down the right road. Conversion: turning around and getting on the right road.

Others of us willfully, rebelliously, choose our own way, knowing full well what we are doing, determined to "get my own way," like the prodigal son in the story that Jesus told (Lk. 15). When, despite all the initial euphoria of being in charge of our own life, we realize that we are on the road to damnation, the obvious thing is simply to turn around and get back on the right road. Conversion: turning around and getting on the road of life.

Conversion is both as simple and significant as stopping, doing an about-face, and walking (or running) down the Road of Life.

Following (Christ)

After conversion, it's follow. Follow Jesus. Following Jesus is the "Yes" that follows the turnaround of conversion. We renounce self-initiative for God-obedience. We renounce clamoring assertions for quiet listening. We watch Jesus work, we listen to Jesus speak, we accompany Jesus into new relationships, odd places and meetings with odd people. Keeping company with Jesus, observing what he does and listening to what he says, develops into a life of answering God, a life of responding to God, which is to say, a life of prayer. For following Jesus is not robotic, lockstep marching in a straight line behind Jesus. The following gets inside us, becomes internalized, gets into our muscles and nerves; it becomes prayer and obedience.

When "following Jesus" is installed as our primary metaphor for living, we are prevented from reducing the Christian life to abstractions that we can manipulate for our own convenience. We are prevented from taking bits and pieces of Jesus' way of life and then using them to go our own way at our own pace. Following Jesus requires that we keep our eyes on Jesus, keep our ears open to Jesus, stick with Jesus. Once we decide to follow Jesus, everything we know and believe about him is harnessed in biblical leather to obedience to him. "Follow" is belief in action. Following Jesus means that our legs and feet are coordinated with our mind and heart. Following Jesus means trusting Jesus to lead the way. We follow because we don't know the way to eternal life, to salvation, to happiness—to any of the "well-known words." But Jesus knows the way—he is the Way—and so we follow Jesus.

In following Jesus, it doesn't take us long to realize that Jesus has no interest in making it easy for us; he doesn't avoid tough climbs or detour around rough terrain; he doesn't put us up in the best hotels. But we also realize that Jesus doesn't take us anyplace that he doesn't first go himself.

Mercy

There is an enormous amount of suffering and injustice and unhappiness in the world. The wounds and the weeping, the rejections and betrayals are constant and sometimes overwhelming. Brutalized, damaged, and beaten up men, women, and children are brought to our attention daily. We see pictures of them, read stories of them, feel sorry for them. But what can we do? We don't know their names, don't even know exactly where they live. Eventually it all gets to be too much. We begin to construct defenses to keep the pain from making us miserable. We find ways to put distance between ourselves and them. We depersonalize them with criticism and blame. Or we develop poses of condescending pity that set us apart, superior to their plight. And then one day we discover in dismay that our self-protecting defenses are shutting us off from people whose names we do know, whose street addresses we are familiar with. It's time for an old prayer to break through our defenses:

Lord have mercy,
Christ have mercy,
Lord have mercy.

"Lord, have mercy on me, so I can have mercy on others." When we respond to the suffering of another by avoidance or indifference or rejection or blame, our ability to love atrophies. Our lives are reduced and darkened. When mercy diminishes, humanity itself diminishes—a most dangerous condition. When hearts harden the color goes out of life. Mercy restores suppleness to the heart and embraces darkness with brightness. Does the pain of childbirth diminish a mother's love for her newborn infant?

Death

Life defines who we are, these complex arrangements of protein and protoplasm, skin and bones, muscle and tissue, blood and water—and, yes, hopes and dreams, words and songs, love and hope, courage and beauty. We are "fearfully and wonderfully made" (Ps. 139:14). Death puts an end to all this. We experience it as an intrusion on a world of wonders, a violation of a holy creation.

But it is not all bad. The death sentence (Gen. 2:17), after all, was given by God, the same God who spoke life into being. Death puts an end to a life of disobedience and sin. It puts an end to pride and pretension. It puts an end to cruel behavior and brutal abuse. It puts an end to betrayal and rejection. "Death is a good thing," wrote poet Alan Dugan; "if we were immortal we would be insufferable."

And it also seems to be a good thing to have limits to our lives, to work under a deadline that can't be postponed. We are not then so apt to squander what is precious. Responding to the Psalmist's "teach us to count our days" (90:12), Martin Luther commented: "Moses wants all of us to become such good arithmeticians!"

The death of Jesus radically reconfigured all this and amalgamated the good and bad of death into a gospel: this death went on public exhibit as the worst that can happen; this death gathered up all death and offered it to God to atone for the sins of the world, the best that can happen. In the tangle of pain and beauty, blasphemy and prayer, humiliation and majesty that composed Jesus' death by crucifixion, God secretly and profoundly worked a new light-filled creation. From that black hill we catch the first rays of the "new heavens and new earth."

Resurrection

The Western world has never been as successful at commodifying the resurrection of Jesus as it has his birth. Christmas is a huge commercial enterprise, Easter only minimally so. Birth we understand, resurrection is beyond us. We all have multiple experiences of birth: we know the mothers, we know the fathers, we cuddle the babies. Resurrection is exclusively God's work; nobody saw it happen; they still don't. Nor could the first witnesses explain it; and we still can't. And if we can't, as we say, "get a handle on it" and find some way to make something of it, we soon lose interest.

Our four Gospel writers all complete their narratives with a story or stories of Jesus' resurrection. They come at it from different directions and provide different details, but one element is common to them all: a sense of wonder, astonishment, surprise. Despite several hints scattered through the Hebrew Scriptures, and Jesus' three explicit statements forecasting his resurrection, when it happened it turned out that no one was expecting it. The first people involved in Jesus' resurrection were totally involved in dealing with death. Now they had to do a complete about-face and deal with life. As they did it, they were suffused with wonder.

The resurrection was not just about Jesus, it was about them (us!). As it turned out, it was a quiet business that took place in a quiet place without publicity or spectators; only the participants were involved. Resurrection is not a road show. Given the way we surround important events with attention-getting publicity and considering that this is the big Gospel news, this is a surprise. Resurrection doesn't need bright lights and amplification; astonishment and wonder are enough to pull us into the resonant new life with Christ.

Eternity

Here's an old story that attempts to give a feel for eternity. In the remote deserts of Mongolia there is a freestanding steel wall that is three feet thick and one thousand feet tall. Once a year an angel comes down with a silk scarf and lightly brushes the top of the wall. When the steel wall has been eroded down to the desert floor, eternity will have just begun.

The story is vivid, but it is wrong. It is wrong because it imagines eternity as merely the prolongation of time as we measure it with our watches and clocks and calendars through our round of days and nights, our months and years. Eternal life is not the endless extension of time but the intensification and purification of "a complete present and presence, of an utterly abiding here and now" (von Hugel). Jesus tells us that eternal life takes place in the present; it is not what we enter into after we die, it is what we enter into now as we believe in Jesus, receiving the gift of life, eternal life (Jn. 5:24–26; 17:3). Eternal life is Jesus' gift of fully real, fully present life.

We have occasional intimations of eternity in the natural course of living. We sometimes say, when we have become unselfconsciously absorbed in what we are doing or seeing, that "we lost all track of time," or "time stood still." Our sense of time as a sequence or succession of intervals measured by a timepiece is obliterated by a very different awareness—presence intensified, an all-pervasive now, real life. But these are only hints of eternity. Eternity is not about time as such; it includes everlastingness but it is primarily about God and all time coming into completion in us as we know and worship God—now and forever.

Covenant

Everything is connected. Butterflies and plankton, dogs and elephants, the traffic emissions in New York and the gardens in London, the debris left on the moon and the vineyards in the Rhône Valley. We find ourselves inextricably woven into an intricate creation web that is absolutely comprehensive; no one and no thing is left out. The ecologists tell us this much and, though it is virtually impossible to imagine, the evidence mounts by the decade and seems irrefutable.

But what about us and God? Field research hasn't yet been funded to put the scientific community to work on the question, but we don't have to wait.

Scripture and devout reflection on Scripture have taken up the question and the answer is the same: everything is connected. Everything in us is connected with everything in God; everything regarding God is connected with everything regarding us. There is nothing of God that does not have something to do with us; there is nothing of us that does not have something to do with God. Covenant is the word used to mark the organic, living connectedness of God and us that makes us a community of God, not disconnected individuals more or less "on our own."

Covenant is frequently misunderstood, and therefore wrongly lived, when it is thought of as a contract. A contract is the normal device by which people agree on an item of mutual interest and bind themselves to mutual responsibilities. It has to do with things (usually involving money) and is regulated and enforced by our legislative and judicial system. But a covenant is not legal but personal; the heart and soul of covenant is promise and obedience, faithfulness and worship. Covenant involves not things but souls and is kept in repair not by fines and jails but by forgiveness and repentance, love and worship. Covenant provides the form and conditions by which we live as God's community. By means of God's covenant with us, his people, we understand and experience how thoroughly personal and absolutely faithful he is in dealing with us in every part of our lives and together as the People of God.

Blessing

By its very nature, life is meant to be shared. Kept to itself, held onto, grasped in a Midas clutch, it diminishes and withers. The zest goes out of it, the spark dulls, the taste goes flat.

Blessing names the overflow of life, the brimming of the cup that spills life's goodness and beauty on anyone who happens to be standing nearby. Blessing is reckless, prodigal, uncalculating. It is generosity with wings.

God blesses. All that God is and has he pours out on us. If we don't know and accept that, we will live badly. There is nothing stingy in God; nothing mean or niggardly. We are born into a lavishly graced existence. At the core of learning how to live well, is learning how to receive, to accept, to appreciate and enjoy gifts. Suspicion, fear, and cynicism incapacitate us from a robust openness to living the blessings.

There is hardly a circumstance in life that is immune from blessings. Our journey of faith as told in the story of Abraham begins with words of blessing (Gn. 12:2–3). Our life of prayer, which keeps us in intimate touch with God's involvement in all the details of our lives and spreads out before us in the Psalms, begins with blessing (Ps. 1:1). Our behavior in the Kingdom as laid out by Jesus in his first teaching sermon begins with eight magnificent blessings (Mt. 5:1–12). And when John of Patmos prepares our imaginations to take in the glorious completion of all things in Christ, he artfully weaves seven blessings into his grand vision (Rev. 1:3; 14:13; 16:15; 19:9; 20:6; 22:7; 22:14).

From beginning to end, this strong, powerful current of God's blessing carries us through everything life can throw at us. We are not only extravagantly blessed, we are now able to bless others in this God-blessed world.

(Holy) Spirit

The term "spirit" is a metaphor in biblical languages. In Hebrew and Greek it simply means "wind" or "breath." It is invisible; we only know it is present by seeing or feeling what it does: blows clouds through the sky, fills the sails of a boat and sends it scudding across a lake, cools our perspiring skin on a hot day, fills our lungs.

When trees are waving wildly we know that a mighty wind is making them dance. Biblically informed men and women, observing the intricacies of creation, the marvels of salvation, and the daily blessings that keep our lives alert in adoration and praise, know that God's wind/breath/spirit is behind it all. The Invisible is behind and gives energy, color, and shape to the visible. It happens all the time; it happens every day: God present and active among us—the Holy Spirit.

Having lost the metaphorical origin of "spirit," we have a serious vocabulary deficit in our daily conversations, in the English language at least. Imagine how our perceptions would change if we eliminated the word spirit from our language and used only wind and breath? Spirit was not "spiritual" for our ancestors; it was sensual. It was the invisible that had visible effects. It was invisible but it was not immaterial. Air has as much materiality to it as a granite mountain: it can be felt, heard, and measured; it provides the molecules for quiet breathing that is part of all life, human and animal, waking and sleeping, the puffs of air used to make words, the gentle breezes that caress the skin, the brisk winds that windmills turn into electricity, the wild hurricanes that tear roofs off barns.

When we add the adjective "holy" to spirit we name the invisible God visibly at work among us, creating and saving and blessing. The Holy Spirit is God's way of being present with us, making us participants in his being and work. It is not in neon, but it's there.

Peace

"Give me a little peace, can't you" we say to someone who is nagging us. We mean "quit bothering me." Peace talks between warring nations involve trying to get them to quit killing one another. *Requiescat in pace* ("rest in peace"), abbreviated to R.I.P., used to be a popular epitaph on gravestones, memorializing the assumption that being dead is the ultimate peaceful state. But until we break the habit of using the word peace in a negative way, we will never get it right.

Peace, God's peace, the "peace of God which passes all understanding" (Phil. 4:7), is not absence but presence, not less hassle but more harmony, harmony between things and people, but mostly people—alert and relational mutuality, personal exchanges of respect and delight. There is nothing lethargic or static about peace; it involves total participation in life at its most vital. It is like a vigorous folk dance, the opposite of lazily sleeping through the ringing of the alarm clock.

When Jesus told his disciples "peace I leave with you," he immediately defined what he meant by breathing the Holy Spirit on them (Jn. 20:21–22). That same Holy Spirit descended upon them some days later in fire and wind, making them highly energetic participants in everything that Jesus had been doing among them. Jesus' gift of peace set them loose in the world and they were soon turning that world upside down (Acts 17:6) as they continued doing Jesus' work of proclaiming and healing, teaching and loving, praying and giving witness to the resurrection.

When we receive God's peace our experience is not of being removed from conflict so that we can live a quiet, undisturbed life on our own terms. No, we are plunged into life on God's terms, the light-filled action of Father, Son, and Holy Spirit in the three-ring circus of salvation.

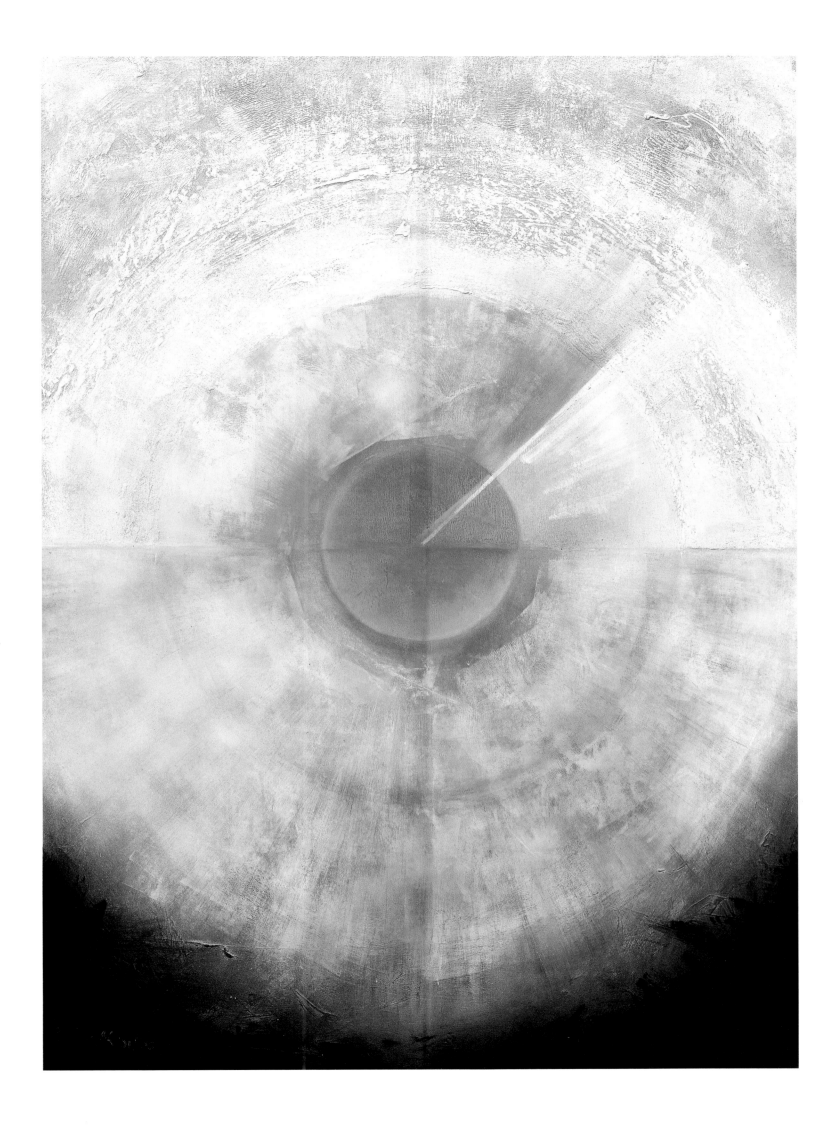

Amen

Amen: "Yes . . . that's right . . . I couldn't have said it better myself." This ancient Hebrew word has entered untranslated into every language spoken by Christians and Jews, Amen. Amen: the magnificent, affirmative word that grounds everything God is and does for us in Christ. Amen is the great affirmation that God most surely is who he has revealed himself to be in Scripture and in Christ. Amen is the thundering affirmation that God does what he has promised to do. Amen is the whispered assurance that nothing can separate us from God's love. Amen is a sister word to faithfulness—God's rock steady, solidly dependable word and presence.

There is necessarily much ambiguity in the life of faith, no less than in life in general. We can't see what is coming. We don't understand the circumstances in which we find ourselves. We are deluged with words and messages, promises and counsel and don't know what or who to believe. We patiently (or impatiently) wait, sometimes for unaccountably long times, to discern our place in the world of salvation. But for those who follow Jesus, both at center and circumference, the word keeps sounding in ears and hearts, a steadying rhythm: Amen . . . Amen . . . Yes . . . Yes.

Jesus frequently used the double Amen ("Amen, amen, I say to you"), often translated, "Truly, truly," to emphasize the utter reliability of what he was saying to his listeners. But he not only said it, he was it, his life, death, and resurrection the good soil in which our lives are planted and grow up every day, exuberant and flourishing into Christ (Eph. 4:16).

Artist's Notes

Love

The fire of love in the heart of the round shape symbolizes the love of God for the world through Christ, which is why there is a crucifix embedded in the painting. Around the flames of love, human love is pictured, love for one another. Together these complementing, embracing forms radiate warmth to the surrounding world.

1 John 4:19 *We love because he first loved us.*

Grace

The Hebrew word *cheen* indicates an inclination, a bending over, a reaching out. This root meaning comes out clearly in the grace of God. It is overwhelming, full of love (red), and precious (gold) because it cost God his only Son, as symbolized by the Cross.

Ephesians 2:5c, 7 *It is by grace you have been saved . . . in Christ Jesus.*

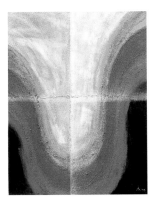

Happiness

The New Testament Greek word for happiness is *chara*, and for grace, *charis*. It shows the close connection in meaning between these two words. Happiness in the biblical sense is a life rooted in God's grace. This joyful experience is expressed here as a crucifix-shaped composition surrounded by colorful shapes that symbolize a multitude of lifted arms.

Philippians 4:4 *Rejoice in the Lord always. I will say it again: Rejoice!*

Holiness

In the Old Testament the Hebrew word for holy is *qadosh*, with the root meaning of "separated." In this painting the illuminated rectangular plane, strongly connected with the surrounding light that symbolizes God, is distinctly separated from the gray area. Separation in holiness is separation for a purpose: to be directed towards one's neighbors, here pictured as white lines that connect the two planes; it is also how God reaches out to humankind.

1 Peter 1:16 *For it is written: "Be holy, because I am holy."*

Wrath

Inspired by the shape of a clenched fist, this painting shows wrath ignited. Such deep anger can also be the result of disappointed love. Red and black together express turbulent emotion, and combined with yellow represent feelings of pain, anger, and fury.

Ephesians 4:26 *"In your anger do not sin:" Do not let the sun go down while you are still angry.*

(un)Righteousness

The red beam that has snapped under the immense pressure of the black, gritty dirt pictures the emotional state of a person who has been broken by unjust oppression.

Isaiah 59:14 *So justice is driven back and righteousness stands at a distance; truth has stumbled in the streets.*

Underneath the red beam we notice a broken white beam, which symbolizes Christ. Through his death God is able and willing to restore the broken person. Such a restoration is pictured in the upright red plane where, in fellowship with God, the restored now treat others with justice.

1 Peter 3:18 *For Christ died for sins once for all, the righteous for the unrighteous, to bring you to God.*

Reconciliation

Generally reconciliation means "to cover," "to restore peace." On earth there is much fighting among people and it leads to suffering, as indicated by the purple color. The vertical crossbar, which symbolizes Christ, restores peace with God for us and covers the earth with light. In the light of this Light people have a task to work as peacemakers.

2 Corinthians 5:18 *All this is from God, who reconciled us to himself through Christ and gave us the ministry of reconciliation.*

Power (of the Evil One)

Dangerous red-hot fire tongs threaten to capture someone and to entangle them in a web of darkness. This leads to great suffering, which is indicated by the purple color. This painting was conceived in the aftermath to the terrorist attack in New York on 11 September 2001.

Colossians 1:13a *For he has rescued us from the dominion of darkness.*

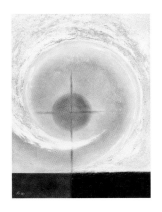

Power (of God)

We cannot consider the power of God in isolation from his Fatherhood, expressed here in the undefined, limitless white that embraces and supports the earth. The black strip to the right below symbolizes death, stopped dead in its tracks by God's power, the cross of Christ.

Psalm 77:14, 15a *You are the God who performs miracles; you display your power among the peoples. With your mighty arm you redeemed your people.*

Sin

The Hebrew word for sin is *chattah* and it means to miss the goal. There is a clear break here between the planes with the beautiful, paradisical colors in order to show that the goal, namely Paradise, has been missed. The break is emphasized by the dark, round shape at the back that symbolizes the results of sin on earth.

1 John 1:8 *If we claim to be without sin, we deceive ourselves and the truth is not in us.*

Forgiveness

This painting expresses the biblical understanding of forgiveness: that through the death of Christ, God wipes out our guilt. We get a second chance, a new start. Knowing that, his forgiven people are called to live a life which also freely "wipes out" guilt. Then life becomes alive (green).

Matthew 6:12 *Forgive us our debts, as we also have forgiven our debtors.*

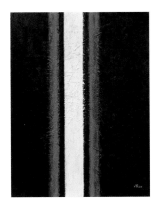

Salvation

The black planes, which symbolize heavy prison doors, are slid apart . . . the Light of freedom breaks the bonds. The vertical red strips are reminiscent of the blood that the Israelites smeared on their door lintels at the time of the Exodus from Egypt. It points to Christ, who has made our salvation possible.

Luke 1:68 *Praise be to the Lord, the God of Israel, because he has come and has redeemed his people.*

Conversion

The Hebrew word *sjubah* means "to turn around, to turn back." The person who has unfastened from life in the dark, who has unhooked from it, can turn around to face God, to face the Light.

Acts 26:17b, 18a *I am sending you to them to open their eyes and turn them from darkness to light.*

Following (Christ)

The rising red line expresses love that follows the way of Christ, who asked his disciples to pick up their cross, to choose life, and to set their eyes on him alone. Christ's way has a light side but at times also leads through the dark; it always has an eternal perspective.

Matthew 16:24 *Then Jesus said to his disciples: "If anyone would come after me, he must deny himself and take up his cross and follow me."*

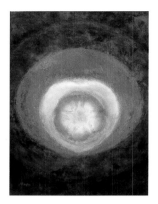

Mercy

The Hebrew word *rechem* refers to the love of a mother for her unborn child. The word for mercy is derived from it and means to be kind, to care for the tender and weak, to have compassion. The large red shape shows God's loving care for vulnerable, little ones. When people live in kindness towards one another, as pictured in the small embracing red shapes at the heart of the larger red area, love flowers on earth.

Luke 6:36 *Be merciful, just as your Father is merciful.*

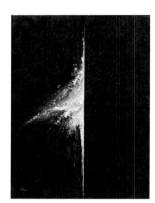

Death

As the black door of death slides open, everlasting Light appears triumphantly!

1 Corinthians 15:54c, 57 *"Death has been swallowed up in victory . . ."*
But thanks be to God! He gives us the victory through our Lord Jesus Christ.

Resurrection

The larger red, arched line pictures the power of the resurrection of Christ from the dead (black mixed with soil). He creates a connection between death and new life (light green). Dark death is not the end; light has the victory. Through this victory a person can rise up to new life with Christ, as symbolized here by the smaller red, arched line.

Romans 6:8 *Now if we died with Christ, we believe that we will also live with him.*

Eternity

Eternity has no beginning and no end. In the painting we see diagonal lines below that reach infinitely far into the past, and diagonal lines above that vanish into an unfathomable future. This present moment on earth is pictured in the middle.

Psalm 90:2 *Before the mountains were born or you brought forth the earth . . . from everlasting to everlasting you are God.*

Covenant

The biblical covenant is more than a legal agreement between people (the interwoven blue shapes). God is a witness to this agreement (the light shape behind the blue). The covenant of God, initiated by him, is pictured here in the mutual embrace between the large light round area and the round blue shape. The predominance of blue in this painting indicates that faithfulness and covenant have a close relationship.

Jeremiah 31:33/Hebrews 8:10 *This is the covenant I will make with the house of Israel . . . I will be their God and they will be my people.*

Blessing

God's blessing is his putting his active, positive favor on a person or object, the receiver of the blessing. We can also intercede on behalf of others and ask God to bless a person or object. This painting pictures the giving and receiving of God's favor as a flowing current.

Numbers 6:24 *The Lord bless you and keep you.*

(Holy) Spirit

The Old Testament Hebrew word *ruach* means spirit, breath, wind; the New Testament Greek word *pneuma* refers particularly to the breath of life; the biblical images associated with the Holy Spirit are fire and wind. In this painting the Holy Spirit is pictured as God's breath of life, which makes Christ known to us, expressed as a crucifix in the fire and wind.

Romans 5:5 *And hope does not disappoint us, because God has poured out his love into our hearts by the Holy Spirit.*

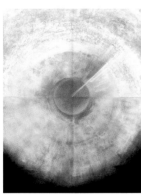

Peace

Peace is more than the absence of war. The Old Testament word *shalom* indicates living in a healthy relationship with God, oneself, and the environment. The heart of the light, round shape here symbolizes the inner person, the white band above pictures God, and the shape below refers to the surrounding world. This simple composition expresses a peaceful, orderly rest (*eirene* in Greek). Through Christ, peace with God and the environment is possible, which is why the cross dominates the composition. The inner peace that results is pictured as a rising sun (the moment of peace in nature). Its gentle light softens the harsh contradictions in our world.

John 14:27 *Peace I leave with you; my peace I give you.*

Amen

"Amen" affirms . . . that something is trustworthy: totally true and secure! The light beam in this sober painting rests on the Cross, which guarantees solid ground. Above it the light green plane symbolizes life—green is the color of life—that flourishes when grounded in a firm base.

2 Corinthians 1:20 *For no matter how many promises God has made, they are "Yes" in Christ. And so through him the "Amen" is spoken by us to the glory of God.*

Acknowledgments

Firstly I want to thank my husband for his patient and loving support in this project. Thanks also to my children, Géran and Gieneke, and Riegonda and Erik, for their warm and enthusiastic interest. I am very grateful to Dolf Hoving, who once again took responsibility for organizing the high-quality slides necessary for printing.

Professor Eugene Peterson wrote the sparkling text for the English edition, and I thank him for adding the dimension of his word paintings to my paintings in acrylic.

I thank my English publishers, Piquant, with Paraclete Press in the USA. In the Netherlands the book is published as *Bijbelwoorden in beeld*.

It is my hope that the exploration of these well-known words in a contemporary visual language will encourage rich and rewarding reflection:

That
As God's love inspires me
To work in the power of his Spirit,
Alive with resurrection life,
Following his way,
Experiencing his mercy,
Overflowing with joy,
I too may become a blessing.
Amen.

ANNEKE KAAI